YOUR KNOWLEDGE HAS VALUE

- We will publish your bachelor's and
  master's thesis, essays and papers

- Your own eBook and book -
  sold worldwide in all relevant shops

- Earn money with each sale

Upload your text at www.GRIN.com
and publish for free

Manü Mohr

About "The Oval Portrait" of Edgar Allan Poe

GRIN Verlag

Bibliografische Information der Deutschen Nationalbibliothek:

Die Deutsche Bibliothek verzeichnet diese Publikation in der Deutschen National-
bibliografie; detaillierte bibliografische Daten sind im Internet über http://dnb.d-
nb.de/ abrufbar.

Dieses Werk sowie alle darin enthaltenen einzelnen Beiträge und Abbildungen
sind urheberrechtlich geschützt. Jede Verwertung, die nicht ausdrücklich vom
Urheberrechtsschutz zugelassen ist, bedarf der vorherigen Zustimmung des Verla-
ges. Das gilt insbesondere für Vervielfältigungen, Bearbeitungen, Übersetzungen,
Mikroverfilmungen, Auswertungen durch Datenbanken und für die Einspeicherung
und Verarbeitung in elektronische Systeme. Alle Rechte, auch die des auszugsweisen
Nachdrucks, der fotomechanischen Wiedergabe (einschließlich Mikrokopie) sowie
der Auswertung durch Datenbanken oder ähnliche Einrichtungen, vorbehalten.

Imprint:

Copyright © 2012 GRIN Verlag GmbH
Druck und Bindung: Books on Demand GmbH, Norderstedt Germany
ISBN: 978-3-656-48620-6

This book at GRIN:

http://www.grin.com/en/e-book/231878/about-the-oval-portrait-of-edgar-allan-poe

Of what in other worlds shall be – and given
In beauty by our God, to those alone
Who otherwise would fall from life and Heaven
Drawn by their heart's passion, and that tone,
That high tone of the spirit which hath striven,
Tho' not with Faith – with godliness – whose throne
With desperate energy 't hath beaten down;
Wearing its own deep feeling as a crown.
(Poe, "Stanzas")

Edgar Allan Poe is one of the most famous and celebrated American writers whose short stories inspired numerous other authors. *The Oval Portrait*, initially titled *Life in Death*, is a revised and shorter version that was published in the *Broadway Journal* in 1845. Although being one of his shortest stories, Poe is able to establish in *The Oval Portrait* a haunting atmosphere of terror. The fate of the beautiful, young woman fascinates the narrator who is entirely taken by the enigmatic painting and the inscrutable circumstances of the lady's death. It is in this way that the author is able to create simultaneously a sense of both mystery and tragedy, and this essay will examine in greater detail how these two elements are combined in order to make up the Gothic mood typical for Poe's writings.

Firstly, I will have a look at the author and his background before providing some general information about this short story. In this case, a biographical approach to *The Oval Portrait* is very enriching and is able to shed light on some aspects, as we will see later on.

Secondly, I will concentrate on the appearance of the mysterious atmosphere in the work, such as the narrator's equivocal reliability, the mansion and its relation to the Gothic, the role of light and darkness, and the open questions. My third point of analysis will be the tragic: how is Poe able to make both the story's narrator and his readers be captivated by such a sad woman's death within less than four pages? To begin with, I will focus on the painter and his obsession with his art, as well as the dilemma whether the latter is inevitably irreconcilable with life. Then the woman's outward appearance, that is her surpassing loveliness, will be linked to what Poe himself says about the role of beauty and horror in his work *Philosophy of Composition*.

Furthermore, James Twitchell's interpretation of *The Oval Portrait* will be taken into account.

Eventually, in the conclusion, it will become clear that even after having read the short story, a reader still remains with the feeling that there is more behind it, yet he or she cannot exactly tell what it is: the ineffable comes into play, showing that Poe's writings represent the apogee of the tales of the macabre in the nineteenth century, and that he deserves to be called 'the master of Gothic fiction'.

Edgar Allan Poe was born in Boston in 1809; his parents have been actors of the Powell's Company, and they died few years later. Thus, he was sent to John Allan, a rich merchant, and his wife Frances, who affectionately accommodated him, treating him like their own son while their own marriage remained childless. In the 1820s, he attended private schools and the University of Virginia before starting a career as a writer. In May 1836, his foster parents have already died, Poe married his 13-year-old cousin Virginia Clemm. His wife played a decisive role in his poems and stories, and she also heavily influenced the writing of *The Oval Portrait*. Given the fact that Virginia was in ill health and suffered from tuberculosis that finally caused her death in 1847, we can see that the hardships, sorrows and deaths which Poe had to endure in his life, sometimes reappear in his works. The loss of his wife could be connected to the death of the beautiful lady in the story, with the author drawing attention to the omnipresent and inescapable death that robbed him of his young bride.

However, it is not only the female character whose tragic fate is explored; so one should not neglect the difficulties that Poe himself encountered during his life. Of course, the loss of his loved ones were significant incidents which must have troubled him a lot, and he never had enough stability or financial security. He often changed his editorial positions, being first employed at the *Southern Literary Messenger*, then at *Burton's Gentleman's Magazine* and eventually the *Broadway Journal* until 1846 (cf Zumbach).

Moreover, Poe tried to found new literary journals several times, for instance *The Penn* and *The Stylus*, yet he has never been successful. During the rest of his life, he was addicted to drugs and to alcohol, with this probably being the reason for having protagonists who are mentally unstable or suffer from other mental illnesses and problems. In *The Oval Portrait*, it is the narrator who is severely wounded, feeling that he is almost in a delirium.

Another connection to Poe's biographical background is the description of the vignette "much in the style of the favorite heads of Sully" (Poe 251). Thomas Sully, a well-known American painter who lived from 1783 to 1872, has made a portrait both of Frances and of John Allen. The picture of Poe's foster mother may have served as a model for the portrait of the woman in the short story.

After his wife's death, the author was engaged twice, but none of these relationships have been long-lasting. Edgar Allan Poe died in 1849 under mysterious circumstances, allegedly from alcoholism, in Baltimore. Although he died at a very young age, he played an influential role in the development of the short story and the invention of the detective story. Thanks to him, the genre of Gothic fiction, to which also belongs *The Oval Portrait*, became famous.

This short story is divided into two parts: it begins with an injured narrator who, together with his valet, wants to pass the night in an untenanted chateau in the Apennines. The latter contemplates attentively the portraits hanging on the walls, and all of a sudden, he discovers another painting that fascinates him because of its "absolute *life-likeliness* of expression" (251). As he is eager to find out more about the beautiful young lady, he consults a book that he has found on the pillow of his bed.

The second part, the 'story in the story', is a direct quotation from this book which explains that the lady was the wife of a well-known painter. He was very talented and insisted on making a portrait of his wife who actually did not want to sit for him at all. Despite her initial refusal, she decides to do him the favour, and her husband begins with his work. However, he gets more and more obsessed with his portrait so that he does not notice that his wife begins to waste away in the dark turret. When he finishes the painting which resembles the woman so much that he cries: "'This is indeed *Life* itself!'" (253), he turns around and realizes that she is dead.

In this last half of the short story, the narrator completely fades into the background. Yet it is him who establishes the mysterious mood at the beginning. The first important thing to notice is that the reader never gets to know where the narrator's wound comes from. He remains a dubious character on whose account we have to rely. The question of his trustworthiness is a controversial one: on the one hand, the text says that he is in a "desperately wounded condition" (250) and almost in a semi-delirious state, which could be an indication of an impaired judgement and memory. Furthermore, he is a first person narrator and involved in the story, which is a cause for distrust, too.

On the other hand, when comparing this version to the earlier one, one gets the impression that Poe rather intended to make his narrator more reliable. In *Life in Death*, the reader gets to know that the narrator has taken opium because of his wound that he got during a fight with bandits. By leaving this paragraph out, the author can both envelop the narrator's story in mystery, and make the reader less suspicious, as having to do with outlaws also casts a damning light on the narrator himself. What is more, opium could indicate that the story is not entirely trustworthy. In *The Oval Portrait*, the narrator delivers comparatively long and detailed descriptions of the chateau and the portrait, by means of which his account seems to be an objective one. But at the same time, we find some hints within the text concerning the narrator that contribute to a mysterious atmosphere. When he says, for example, that "[w]hy I did this [closing the eyes] was not at first apparent even to my own perception" (251) and a few lines later "that my fancy, shaken from its half slumber, had mistaken the head for that of a living person", this points at a reason for the reader to question the narrator's credibility, as the latter himself admits that his story may contain some faults.

The abandoned mansion creates an arcane and eerie atmosphere, being a 'typical requisite in the tradition of the Gothic', so to speak. The narrator describes it as "one of those piles of commingled gloom and grandeur which have so long frowned among the Apennines" (250). Two figures of speech are striking here: first, the alliteration in "gloom and grandeur"; second, the personification of the chateau. To say that the latter frowns like someone who is angry or dissatisfied, makes it seem repellent, dark and mysterious. The fact that nobody lives there fits into this image, too.

The narrator and his valet have chosen the smallest apartment of the building which is richly decorated, "yet tattered and antique". On the walls, there are tapestries, armorial trophies, and modern paintings. As the narrator thinks that the number of the paintings is "an unusually great" one, he already draws attention to the possibility that something might be wrong with them and the mansion in general. The architecture is "bizarre", and the "very many nooks" let us think of an enchanted, labyrinthine house.

The allusion to Mrs. Radcliffe at the beginning of the short story has to be seen in this context. Ann Radcliffe, who lived from 1764 to 1823, was an English author who became famous for her works of Gothic Romance fiction. These novels often have as a setting gloomy, eldritch castles, as it is the case in *The Mysteries of Udolpho* that was published in 1794.

In *The Oval Portrait*, the narrator admires the portraits and the furniture of the chateau, suggesting that it is due to his delirium that he is interested in the first. He sees the young lady's picture only incidentally by moving the candelabrum. Poe uses light and darkness to make up the haunting mood: the narrator "bade Pedro to close the heavy shutters of the room – since it was already night – to light the tongues of a tall candelabrum". He reads in the book until midnight, but then he changes the candelabrum's position "as to throw its rays more fully upon the book". It is this movement of the light that makes the narrator see another painting he has not recognized before. As it "had hitherto been thrown into deep shade" (251), the beautiful woman's portrait appears in the room almost like of its own volition. Now it is in "vivid light", but in contrast to this, after having recovered from the shock caused by the realism of the woman, the narrator sees that the details in the painting "melted into the vague yet deep shadow". That could be interpreted as the dark, melancholy aura encompassing the beautiful lady, and as an omen of her early death. Before the narrator starts to read the description of the portrait, he moves the candelabrum in order to make it disappear in the dark again.

Darkness also pervades the room in which the woman sat for the painter, "where the light dripped upon the pale canvas only from overhead" (252). It is associated with a negative, oppressive atmosphere foreboding the unhappy ending. The little bit of light in the turret-chamber "which fell so ghastlily [...] withered the health and the spirits of his bride"; so the light has already assumed the scary characteristic of darkness.

Besides the portrait's composition and the lighting conditions of the chateau, there are some more foreshadowing aspects contributing to a mysterious mood. When the narrator discovers the picture of the woman, it is not mainly her beauty that strikes him, but "I had found the spell of the picture in an absolute *life-likeliness* of expression" (251). After having read the short story, we can understand this as the lady's soul and spirit which are caught in the painting – as if she was somehow alive in it.

Furthermore, in the book the narrator reads it is said that "evil was the hour when she saw, and loved, and wedded the painter" (252). The inversion at the beginning of the sentence emphasises that her marriage will cause her death, and the fast succession of incidents make the lady's fate seem predetermined and inevitable. Finally, we are told that "[i]t was thus a terrible thing for this lady to hear the painter speak of his desire to pourtray [sic] even his young bride" - nevertheless, she ignores her own feelings in order to please her husband. With this conflict being introduced, the reader anticipates that either the problem has to be resolved, or it will lead to a disastrous ending.

In addition, Poe creates a mysterious atmosphere by leaving many questions unanswered, which is, besides brevity and a beginning in medias res, a common feature of the short story. It is the reader who has to fill these gaps with his or her own imagination; this is another reason why there seems to remain something ineffable, a denouement that is never completely achieved.

In the following, I will deal with the tragic elements occurring in *The Oval Portrait*. A decisive point is the painter's obsession with art, and the question whether the latter is always incompatible with life.

The lady's husband is described as "passionate, studious, austere": his art means everything to him, so the text repeats a few lines later that he is "passionate", but also a "wild and moody man". By depicting him as a rather unappealing and eccentric character, Poe both sets him in contrast to his wife, and can explain the painter's indifference towards her.

It is also said that he has "already a bride in his Art", which means that his love for painting is stronger than the love for his wife. Only due to this attitude, the painter's obsession can exist and do mischief. When he is about to finish the portrait, he even locks himself and the woman up in the gloomy turret nobody is allowed to enter because he does not want to be disturbed. He has "grown wild with the ardor of his work" and cannot think but at his painting. People who have seen it have complimented the painter on the resemblance, and mistaken this for a love proof. In reality, however, he does not care at all about his wife and her feelings, "turn[ing] his eyes from the canvas rarely, even to regard the countenance of his wife".

After the last brushstroke, the painter is very enthusiastic about his portrait, exclaiming "'This is indeed *Life* itself!'" (253). But when he looks at the woman, he has to see that she has died. Edgar Allan Poe tries to show that the relationship between art and life is difficult and ultimately life-consuming. In *The Oval Portrait,* the painter is like one possessed and does not really love his wife. He is an artist who is both creating and destroying: he draws a wonderful picture of the woman, but the price she has to pay for it is high. Her husband becomes her murderer because it is only his art he is interested in.

Yet from the very beginning, we get to know that the lady "dread[s] only the pallet and brushes and other untoward instruments which deprived her of the countenance of her lover" (252). She is aware of having to compete with art for his attention, and at the same time she also understands that her husband is not neglecting her out of maliciousness or on purpose. His all-consuming passion is simply too great, so it is the mere image of his wife that he confuses with the real person. She gets paler and weaker every day, and the painter's desire to immortalize her ironically makes her fade away. The woman is reduced to an object which serves as a model for a wife the artist intends to create and preserve. Thus, it becomes clear that the two passions, love and art, are not able to subsist simultaneously.

The second aspect where tragedy comes into play is the death of the beautiful lady. In the text, she is twice described as "a maiden of rarest beauty, and not more lovely than full of glee". She has married the painter for love, but her affection was not returned. Moreover, the narrator reads that she has been a very amiable, cheerful person: "all light and smiles, and frolicksome [sic] as the young fawn: loving and cherishing all things". These character traits make the woman appear debonaire and likeable in the eyes of a reader. Therefore, her death is all the more deplorable.

Even though she is tormented and ignored by her husband, the lady is obediently doing what the painter demands, never complaining, but "smil[ing] on and on [...], because she saw that the painter, (who had high renown,) took a fervid and burning pleasure in his task". These lines clearly show that the author has set the painter and his wife in contrast to each other. Whereas the artist is the active character who manipulates his wife, follows his passion and creates the portrait, the woman remains passive until the end. In spite of being the main character and the centre of attention in the short story, she is only observed by others. In the book, it is also said that "she was humble and obedient, and sat meekly for many weeks". This prevents her from telling her husband about her innermost feelings; but when she agreed to let her husband make a portrait of her, she was convinced that is was her duty and the right thing to do.

In *The Philosophy of Composition,* Poe reflects about how to write a good poem, taking as an example the creation of "The Raven". Although he does not explicitly say that his ideas can be transferred to short stories, too, I think that they are also enriching when examining *The Oval Portrait,* as this lyric and narrative text have many common generic features. Both display the reduction and compression of a subject-matter, structural complexity, and even the principle of repetition appears in the short story, in that the book says for two times that the woman is "a maiden of rarest beauty".

In terms of the best length, Poe thinks "that there is a distinct limit, as regards length, to all works of literary art – the limit of a single sitting" (1461) in order to produce an effect. The latter has to make "the work *universally* appreciable", and according to him, it is Beauty which is the most suitable topic. Another important feature also present in *The Oval Portrait* is "Passion, or the excitement of the heart", and the tone has to be melancholic and sad. To achieve this, the author combines Death, the most melancholic topic, with Beauty: "the death, then, of a beautiful woman is, unquestionably, the most poetical topic in the world" (1463). Here Poe believes that it has been the lady's beauty that became her sentence of death.

In the Gothic tradition, to be a beautiful woman means to have a fragile and gracile appearance, and to be of a pale skin. Though the woman in the short story has already been described as "a maiden of rarest beauty" (252) from the beginning, she more and more approaches the ideal of female beauty. The longer she poses and smiles for the painter in the dark turret, the weaker and paler she gets. This is the reason why the author often associates sickness with loveliness.

While the lady's health declines, her husband's obsession with the portrait increases, completely ignoring the need of his wife. In the end, he becomes her murderer who will have to assume responsibility for his terrible act. However, it is also clear that the woman's death was by no means intentional because it was simply the passion which has overwhelmed the artist. He wanted to immortalize both himself as a painter, and the beauty of his wife, knowing that nothing can last forever. To make his dream come true, he has taken the woman's life and enclosed it in the painting: "the tints which he spread upon the canvas were drawn from the cheeks of her who sate beside him". This transfer from an inanimate picture to one that strikes the narrator with its life-likeliness leads to another aspect which establishes the tragic atmosphere in this short story, that is the passage from life to death and James Twitchell's idea of vampirism linked to it.

In his essay "Poe's 'The Oval Portrait' and the Vampire Motif", he implies that artists and their works 'suck the life out' of the objects or persons they depict, exactly as vampires, according to the myth, suck out the blood of their victims, who themselves will become vampires. First, Twitchell draws attention to the fact that the story's former title, *Life in Death*, has even more emphasised "the long, horrid history of the vampire" (388). Also in Poe's other tales similar themes can be found: in his short story *Ligeia*, he describes this woman according to the Gothic ideal, as she is also pretty, slender, and pale. Obsession with Ligeia's perfection, as well as death, are subjects which Poe accentuates, too.

Furthermore, the author disguises the vampire motif because he "dropped the epigraph [...] 'He is alive and would speak if he were not observing the vow of silence' – which has vampiric undertones" (392). Twitchell is convinced that these facts show that in the short story "art is the love, art itself is involved in the transfer of vitality; the process of creation is vampiric" (393). The artist is equalled with a vampire who has to murder in order to stay alive, with this myth being able to show the dangers of art which can also kill.

To sum up, we have seen that in *The Oval Portrait*, the author links mysterious and tragic elements to illustrate his idea of destructive obsession leading to the death of the beautiful woman in the painting.

The most crucial aspect concerning mystery is that this short story belongs to the tradition of Gothic fiction, and the first part of the story told by a homodiegetic narrator aims at establishing an uncanny mood. The abandoned chateau is a typical setting of Gothic works, whose gloomy atmosphere is underlined by the employment of changes between light and darkness.

Moreover, the story makes the reader continue to reflect about it, in that it is really fascinating and capturing: there are questions remaining unanswered until the end, for instance what exactly has happened to the ominous narrator, whose name we never get to know, or where his injury comes from. We could ask ourselves how the painter has reacted to the discovery of his wife's death, as well as what the narrator does after having read the book. Thus, there will always be an uncertainty about the story that cannot be dissipated, with this ineffability being an influential factor for mystery.

When Poe writes about the incompatibility of art and life, he singles out what he considers to be the most tragic subject: a beautiful woman's death. In *The Philosophy of Composition*, the life-taking aspect which causes sadness has been compared to a vampire's act of blood-sucking by James Twitchell.

The Oval Portrait deals with the suffering of the woman caused by her husband's obsession with his art. The latter takes precedence over the love for his wife, so the portrait and the real person cannot be alive at the same time. As I have indicated at the beginning, the death of loved ones is a recurrent subject in Poe's stories being rooted in the tragic experiences of his own life. Therefore, this short story is also a psychological one, and Twitchell even writes that he considers it as "Poe's most sophisticated handling of the vampire motif, now used not to describe eccentric love, but rather the process of artistic creation" (392).

10

Bibliography

Primary Source:
Poe, Edgar Allan. "The Oval Portrait". *Edgar Allan Poe. Selected Writings*. Ed. David Galloway.
Harmondsworth: Penguin Books, 1980.

Secondary Sources:
Galloway, David. Introduction. *Edgar Allan Poe. Selected Writings*. By Galloway.
Harmondsworth: Penguin Books, 1980. 9-46.
Poe, Edgar Allan. "Ligeia". *Edgar Allan Poe. Selected Writings*. Ed. David Galloway.
Harmondsworth: Penguin Books, 1980.
– – – "Stanzas". *Edgar Allan Poe. Selected Writings*. Ed. David Galloway.
Harmondsworth: Penguin Books, 1980.
– – – "The Philosophy of Composition". *The Norton Anthology of American
Literature*. New York: Norton, 1989. 1459-67.
Twitchell, James. "Poe's 'The Oval Portrait' and the Vampire Motif". *Studies in Short Fiction* 14
(1977): 387-93.
Zumbach, Frank. *Edgar Allan Poe*. München: Deutscher Taschenbuch Verlag, 1999.

http://itech.fgcu.edu/faculty/wohlpart/alra/poe.htm (21.12.2011)
http://pphsenglish332.wikispaces.com/The+Oval+Portrait+by+Edgar+Allan+Poe (21.12.2011)
http://poestories.com/biography.php (27.12.2011)
http://www.online-literature.com/ann-radcliffe/ (28.12.2011)